THE SUSTAINABLE BUSINESS WORKBOOK

WASTE ELIMINATION

Jonathan T. Scott and Walter R. Stahel

Greenleaf
PUBLISHING

© 2013 by the Center for Industrial Productivity and Sustainability, Jonathan T. Scott, and the European Foundation for Management Development.

Published by Greenleaf Publishing Limited
Aizlewood's Mill
Nursery Street
Sheffield S3 8GG
UK
www.greenleaf-publishing.com

Typeset and Cover by OKS Prepress Services, Chennai, India
Printed in the UK on environmentally friendly, acid-free paper
from managed forests by CPI Group (UK) Ltd, Croydon

FSC
www.fsc.org

MIX
Paper from
responsible sources
FSC® C013604

British Library Cataloguing in Publication Data:
A catalogue record for this book is available from the British Library.

ISBN-13: 978-1-906093-84-6 [paperback]
ISBN-13: 978-1-909493-07-0 [electronic]

Before you begin...

Whether you are undertaking the requirements of this workbook for your own purposes or with the intent of completing a certification course in sustainable development, the following information should be of help.

The companion text for this publication is *The Sustainable Business: A Practitioner's Guide to Achieving Long-Term Profitability and Competitiveness* (2nd edition). Please note that the seven sections that comprise the companion text (Preparation, Processes, Preservation, People, Place, Product and Production) correspond to the similarly titled sections of this publication.

Read the companion text thoroughly before beginning this workbook.

Many of the subject areas that comprise sustainability are inseparable from one another. For example, certain aspects of *Place* may overlap into *Production*, and so on. This can be confusing when trying to determine where and how to place the information you collect. In such cases, use your best judgement. Accurately measuring and recording the data you are required to collect, and being consistent with its placement, is more important than choosing the category in which it will be placed.

Similarly, the data estimation requirements set forth in this publication may not fit perfectly with the uniqueness of your business, its product, or the environment in which your business operates. Again, do the best you can to meet the highest of standards. Although all of the requirements laid out in this workbook must be met, feel free to modify some of them in order to achieve the intended result: the elimination of waste.

If you have any questions, turn to your waste-elimination team for answers. One of the aims of this course is to promote self-learning, self-development and self-discovery, all of which are best achieved by resolving your own problems. You should:

- *Believe in your creativity.* If you have the right attitude and think you can be innovative and successful, chances are that you will be.

- *Encourage nonconformity.* Allow team members to express different viewpoints.

- *Reach out beyond your specialization.* Use other people (perhaps in different departments) to expand upon ideas and assumptions.

- *Ask 'Why?'* Don't accept that things have to be done the way that they've always been done. Search for more than one right answer or one way to do things.

- *Take the time to think.* Step back, think, play around with ideas, and grow.

- *Don't be afraid of trial and error.* Making a few mistakes is often a path to success.[1]

We hope you find the process of completing this workbook informative and profitable! Good luck!

---

1 Adapted from Roger von Oech, *A Kick in the Seat of the Pants*, Harper & Row, New York, 1986.

The 7-P Model

(The **ROADMAP** to Sustainability)

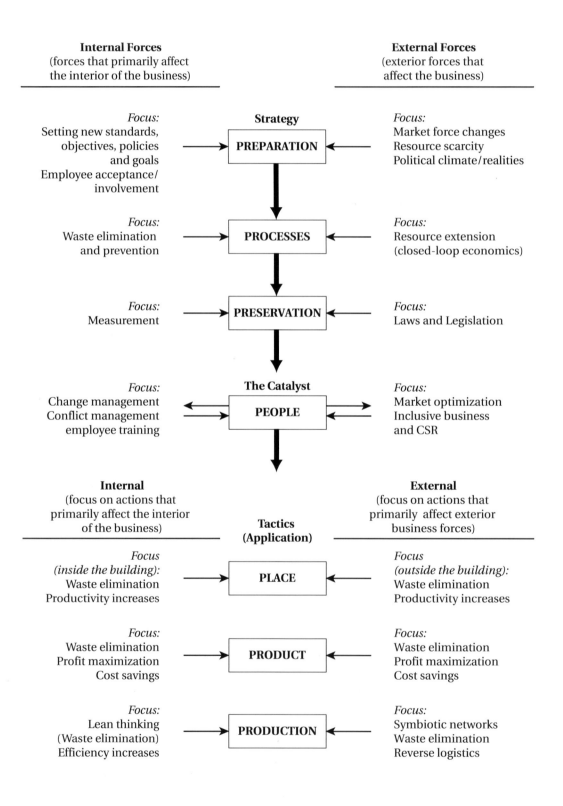

Internal Forces
(forces that primarily affect
the interior of the business)

External Forces
(exterior forces that
affect the business)

Focus:
Setting new standards,
objectives, policies
and goals
Employee acceptance/
involvement

Strategy

PREPARATION

Focus:
Market force changes
Resource scarcity
Political climate/realities

Focus:
Waste elimination
and prevention

PROCESSES

Focus:
Resource extension
(closed-loop economics)

Focus:
Measurement

PRESERVATION

Focus:
Laws and Legislation

Focus:
Change management
Conflict management
employee training

The Catalyst

PEOPLE

Focus:
Market optimization
Inclusive business
and CSR

Internal
(focus on actions that
primarily affect the interior
of the business)

External
(focus on actions that
primarily affect exterior
business forces)

**Tactics
(Application)**

*Focus
(inside the building):*
Waste elimination
Productivity increases

PLACE

*Focus
(outside the building):*
Waste elimination
Productivity increases

Focus:
Waste elimination
Profit maximization
Cost savings

PRODUCT

Focus:
Waste elimination
Profit maximization
Cost savings

Focus:
Lean thinking
(Waste elimination)
Efficiency increases

PRODUCTION

Focus:
Symbiotic networks
Waste elimination
Reverse logistics

The benefits of working through the step-by-step approach to sustainability

If you follow the approach in *The Sustainable Business* and this Workbook, you will find a number of benefits to you and your organization. These include:

Knowledge and understanding

- Increase your awareness of business/management issues and the relationship these issues have with long-term thinking and action (sustainability) in regards to profits, cost-savings, waste elimination, resource optimization and job security/creation,
- Better understand financial value, organizational value and social value,
- Improve your comprehension of applied sustainable practices in both 'blue collar' and 'white collar' settings, and
- Develop the ability to identify, measure and analyze sustainability-based practices and strategies in a work environment.

Subject-specific skills

- Evaluate, synthesize and apply tools for implementing sustainable business practices,
- Measure and analyze sustainable initiatives,
- Be able to identify direct and indirect costs associated with sustainable practices (or the lack of sustainable practices),
- Increase your ability to identify and capitalize upon basic best practices (benchmarking).

Personal and transferable skills

- Improve your ability to plan, measure, manage and lead sustainability-orientated concepts and practices in a real work environment alongside others as part of a team,
- Learn how to produce results and enable others to produce results.

PREPARATION

... the act of making ready (i.e. putting or setting in order in advance of an act or purpose). Before beginning the sustainability process it's important to: (1) learn what sustainability entails, (2) articulate why the pursuit of it is important, and (3) establish the groundwork that will instil both managers and non-management employees with enthusiasm, answers and support. Without this foundation, most attempts at sustainability are prone to confusion, suspicion, disorganization and dwindling motivation – as well as wasted time and efforts.

Energy

External: Market price assessment

1. Create a graph similar to the one below and record the past, present and estimated future market prices of the various forms of energy used by your business.

Energy prices

	Unit of measurement	Current cost per unit	Cost 5 yrs ago	Cost 10 yrs ago	% increase	Estimated cost 5 years from now
Electricity						
Fuel oil						
Natural gas						
Petrol						
Other						

Internal: Costs assessment

2. Create a graph similar to the one below and record your business's total energy costs.

Energy consumption

	Unit of measurement	Amount used	Yearly total cost	Cost 5 yrs ago	Cost 10 yrs ago	% increase	Estimated cost 5 years from now
Electricity							
Fuel oil							
Natural gas							
Petrol							
Other							
TOTAL							

Raw materials or system inputs

External: Market cost assessment

3. Create a graph similar to the one below and record the current price and estimated future market price of select raw materials used by your business. (Note: code words or letters substituted for the names of raw materials can be used to maintain confidentiality.)

Raw material (or system input) costs

Raw material	Unit of measurement	Current cost per unit	Cost 5 yrs ago	Cost 10 yrs ago	% increase	Estimated cost 5 years from now
Water						

Internal: Cost assessment

4. Create a graph similar to the one below and record your business's raw material or system input costs. (Note: code words or letters substituted for the names of raw materials can be used.)

Raw material (or system input) costs

Raw material	Unit of measurement	Amount used	Transport costs	Cost of storage	Cost of handling	Cost of cleanup	Cost of disposal	Total annual cost
Water								
TOTAL								

Briefly describe the three costs (purchase, operating, disposal) associated with each of your raw materials. How can you reduce these costs? (Note: code words or letters substituted for the names of raw materials can be used to maintain confidentiality.)

Waste disposal costs

5. Create a graph similar to the one below. Record your business's annual waste disposal costs.

Total internal annual waste

Types of waste	Unit of measurement	Total amount disposed	Disposal costs			% increase	Est. cost in 5 yrs
			Current	5 yrs ago	10 yrs ago		
Liquid							
Physical							
Gases							
Financial							
Other							

Changes in waste legislation

6. Using the examples in Chapter 1: 'Changes in waste legislation' (in the course text) as a starting point, list any waste and disposal laws that currently affect your business.

7. Next to each law, describe any changes that may be imposed in the future (for example: could the laws become stricter? If so, how?).

8. Describe any current trends that could influence pending or possible future waste disposal legislation. Explain the reasons why such laws could be imposed and the effect each new law would have on your business.

Changes in environmental laws

9. List the environmental laws that currently affect your business. Next to each law, acknowledge any foreseen future changes that may be imposed (for example: could these laws become stricter? If so, how?).

10. Describe any pending or possible future environmental legislation that could affect your business – as well as the reasons why such laws could be imposed.

Raw material procurement

11. List and describe your business's weaknesses in terms of resource scarcity (e.g. raw materials, labour, etc…). Include possible solutions for each.

12. List any additional risk factor problems your business could face in terms of its required resources. Risk factors can include: changes in legislation, climate change, the distance the resources travel (and/or the methods of travel), the origins of the resources (political risk), etc. Describe possible solutions for each.

Changes in customer expectations and demands

13. What do your employees currently think about sustainability? Explain.

14. Briefly describe your customer's thoughts regarding sustainability.

15. What does your business hope to achieve by adopting sustainable business practices?

16. How will you inform your employees about your plans to adopt sustainable practices? How will you involve them?

17. How will you inform your customers about your plans? How will you involve them?

Establishing new policies and objectives

18. Define the word 'quality' *in measurable terms* as it pertains to:
    • Your business,
    • Your product,
    • Sustainability,
    • Your employees, and,
    • Your customers.

19. State your business's 'Sustainable Development' vision, mission statement and objectives.

20. Briefly explain the short-term and long-term goals you will establish in order to achieve your new objectives. Use your definitions of quality and measurement to describe how you plan to implement your new policies (including rewards and punishments).

PROCESSES

A *process* is defined as: (1) a series of progressive, interrelated steps or actions from which an end result is attained, or (2) a prescribed procedure or a method of conducting affairs. Either way, processes form the belief systems, philosophies or thought patterns that constitute the work environments in which goods and services are manufactured (seen from this angle, a business process can also be referred to as a 'business model' or 'the way we do things around here'). Most practitioners agree that for any business process to function properly, total commitment from all involved is mandatory. Success is also reliant upon a perfect fit between the process, its product and the business's customers.

Exterior

Cooperative networks

1. Using Chapter 7 of the course text as a guide, estimate how waste can be eliminated in your business by establishing a cooperative network with the following:
   - A supplier,
   - A competitor,
   - A business in a different industry.
2. List and explain the advantages and disadvantages involved.

Interior

Lean thinking

3. Using Chapter 8 of the course text as a guide (specifically, the nine common forms of waste listed), contact several of your customers to determine their definition of waste and how what they see as waste can be eliminated in your products and/or services.
4. Describe the advantages and/or disadvantages of following through with your customer's suggestions.

PRESERVATION

Preservation is defined as:

- The process of keeping something in existence,
- To keep up or maintain something,
- The act of protecting or safeguarding something from harm or injury,
- Keeping possession of, or retaining, what currently exists.

Any way it's looked at, preservation is not about standing still. In a business context, sustainability demands that two forms of preservation take place. The first is *internal* and involves the collection and analysis of real-time measurement in production processes and product use. The second form is *external* and includes keeping ahead of laws and legislation, industry improvements, directives from customers (e.g. 'scorecards' insisting that packaging or toxins be reduced), disruptive trends, and other forms of change.

External measurement

Laws and legislation

1. Using the 'waste and environmental laws and legislation' data you collected in the *Preparation* section of this workbook, explain how your business will comply with the laws you mentioned as well as how your business will measure and record compliance.

2. Explain how your business will educate its employees so that they understand what full compliance involves. How will you provide ongoing feedback so your employees know they are working within the law?

3. Is it in the best interests of your business to exceed current standards or laws? Explain.

Internal measurement

Measurement: setting goals and targets

4. Using the data collected for the energy and raw material (or system input) cost lists in the *Preparation* section of this workbook, explain:

   a. How does your business measure and record its raw materials or system input costs.

   b. How often does your business record its raw material or system input costs (e.g. in real time, every 15 minutes, daily …?).

   c. How does your business display this data so as to provide ongoing feedback for employees.

5. How can the desired results to the above questions be optimized?

6. Describe any new standards, goals or targets your business will establish that are specifically designed to eliminate and prevent waste (e.g. electricity use will decrease by 25% in 3 months, plastic scrap will decrease by 17% in 6 weeks, human error or accidents will be reduced by 50%, etc. …).

7. Did your employees help set the new standards and targets? What is their overall reaction to them?

8. Describe the role the different departments of your business will play in achieving your new goals.

PEOPLE

Sustainability is not a technological issue. At its core it's a behavioural issue and as such it is dependent upon teamwork, cooperation and motivation. For sustainable practices to take root and produce results, every employee – whether he or she is a cleaner, a production line worker or an administrator – (as well as paying customers) must contribute to the process. No matter what level or experience a person has, everyone has the potential to discover a sustainable path that has been overlooked. Just as important, any employee has the ability to add that final jolt of effort that avoids failure and promotes success. Understanding the importance of people in all phases of the sustainability process is therefore necessary to ensure that a thorough and combined effort on all fronts is made.

Simply put, people are a business's ultimate competitive advantage.

Employee education and involvement

1. Explain how your business will educate and implement its 'Sustainable Development' measures using the nine 'team creation' suggestions listed and described in Chapter 16. Present your answer in the order of the nine suggestions given.

Assessment of future human resource requirements

2. Briefly describe the future human resource requirements of your business and how you plan to address these requirements. Human resource requirement issues can include (but are not limited to):
   - Labour and/or skills shortages,
   - Employee training and education needs,
   - 'Age curve' concerns (e.g. dealing with an aging workforce),
   - Dealing with a multi-cultural workforce.

Assessment of future customer markets

3. Briefly describe the human aspects of your business's future customer markets. Issues that fall within this subject area include, but are not limited to:
   - Customer demands (in terms of sustainability),
   - How your business, its methods and its products measure up against the sustainable activities of competitors,
   - How your business can actively (and successfully) involve its customer base in its waste elimination and prevention objectives.

Job security and job creation

4. Will your business's waste elimination efforts result in job security or the creation of new jobs? Explain your answer.

PLACE

Whether in an office, a factory, a store or a home, most work is conducted in buildings – and the vast majority of the world's buildings are problematic. In some countries, buildings consume more than 68% of all electricity produced, account for over 39% of the nation's energy demands, and are responsible for contributing 38% to the country's total carbon dioxide emissions. Equally as unsettling, it's not uncommon for indoor pollution levels to be two to five times higher (occasionally 100 times higher) than outdoor levels due to dust and fumes from interior building materials, cleaning solutions, production processes, central heating and cooling systems, radon gas, pesticides, paint, glue, carpets and so on. In the USA alone, nationwide building-related productivity losses and illnesses resulting from toxins can cost businesses $60 billion annually. Eliminating these expenses is therefore fundamental to the sustainability process.

Note: Waste associated with 'Place' refers to that which comes from the use and functioning of a building or an area within a building, not from production processes.

Exterior waste elimination and prevention

1. List and describe the actions your business can take to eliminate and prevent *exterior* building and/or workplaces waste in your business.

    *   Describe the costs involved for each action,
    *   Record the estimated payback period (in terms of time and ROI) for each action,
    *   Record the estimated *annual* cost savings of each action.

Interior waste elimination and prevention

2. List and describe the actions your business can take to eliminate and prevent *interior* building and/or workplaces waste in your business.

    *   Describe the costs involved for each action,
    *   Record the estimated payback period (in terms of time and ROI) of each action,
    *   Record the estimated *annual* cost savings of each action.

Unforeseen results after implementation

3. List and describe any unforeseen results of the actions taken (above). For example: Will employees object? How will motivation be maintained? How will you resolve problems? How will you measure increases or decreases in employee absenteeism? How will you measure employee performance increases or decreases? How will you react to increases or decreases in sales?

Waste elimination (by unit)

4. Create a graph similar to the one below and record the combined interior and exterior amounts of building-related waste that your business estimates it can eliminate annually.

Types of waste	Unit of measurement	Total amount eliminated (by unit) annually
Liquid:		
Solid:		
Gases:		
Other:		

Under each category (liquid, solid, etc.) list the name or types of waste you estimate will be eliminated.

Waste elimination: cost savings

5. Create a graph similar to the one below. Using the interior and exterior waste data you have collected, enter the amount of estimated annual cost savings (in euros) that your business can expect to save. (Note: *local application* refers to the estimated amount saved in your business or department alone. *Company-wide application* refers to the estimated savings if the applied savings were adopted at all your business's similar departments or subsidiaries.)

Resource	Estimated total annual savings (€) (*local application*)	Estimated total annual savings (€) (*company-wide application*)
Electricity	€	€
Oil/diesel	€	€
Gas	€	€
Water	€	€
Other	€	€

Lessons learned

6. List and describe the challenges and difficulties your business encountered before, during and after the implementation of its PLACE-orientated waste elimination and prevention ideas as well as any of the changes made to the initial policies, training programs, feedback displays and reward systems that you originally set. Did you have to modify your Sustainable Development program after you started it? If so, what was changed and how did you change it?

PRODUCT

Because of the vast quantities of materials and energy that most products require, not to mention the huge amounts of waste they produce while they're being manufactured, making products more efficient (and more efficiently) is crucial to reducing the costs of running a sustainable business. To be sure, redesigning products and the methods used to make them is time-consuming and arduous; however, many practitioners attest that it can also be the most financially rewarding.

Raw materials and system inputs

Using the 'Ten ways to minimize product waste' (described in Chapter 20) as a template, respond to the following:

Interior waste: elimination and prevention

1. Briefly describe the actions your business will take to eliminate and prevent the *interior* waste associated with your product or service in accordance with each of the 'Ten ways to minimize product waste'. (Note: *interior waste* can include actions taken by suppliers.)

    *   Describe the costs involved for each action,
    *   Record the estimated payback period (in terms of time and ROI) for each action,
    *   Record the estimated *annual* cost savings of each action.

    Note: If your business is an information services provider, a financial institute, an insurance provider, or other form of service business, determine its system input costs in the form of:

    *   Fraud, lawsuits, etc.,
    *   Risk, damages, unnecessary financial loss, etc.,
    *   Weaknesses or redundancies in processing systems, documentation, billing…,
    *   Poor investments,
    *   Human error/accidents,
    *   Customer relations, customer complaints, etc.

Exterior waste: elimination and prevention

2. Briefly describe the actions your business will take to eliminate and prevent *exterior* waste associated with your product or service in accordance with each of the 'Ten ways to minimize product waste'. (Note: *external costs* can include customer-related actions that reduce product or service waste.)

    *   Describe the costs involved for each,
    *   Record the estimated payback period (in terms of time and ROI) of each action,
    *   Record the estimated *annual* cost savings of each action.

    Note: If your business is an information services provider, a financial institute, an insurance provider, or other form of service business, place the appropriate applicable subject areas below under the 'Raw materials' section of your graphs and fill in the data accordingly:

    *   Fraud.
    *   Risk.
    *   Weaknesses in processing systems, documentation, billing, and so on.
    *   Poor investments.
    *   Employee training (or lack thereof).
    *   Customer relations (or lack thereof).
    *   etc…

Waste elimination (by unit)

3. Create a graph similar to the one below and record the combined *product*-related interior and exterior waste data that your business estimates it can eliminate annually.

Types of waste	Unit of measurement	Total amount eliminated (by unit) annually
Liquid:		
Solid:		
Gases:		
Other:		

Under each category (liquid, solid, etc.) list the specific forms or types of waste being eliminated.

Overall material (or system) cost savings

4. Create a graph similar to the one below and record the cost savings derived from your *product*-related waste elimination actions. 'Direct estimated costs' refers to the purchase cost of raw materials. 'Indirect estimated costs' refers to the cost of handling, processing and disposing of materials. (Note: code words substituted for the names of raw materials can be used to maintain confidentiality.)

Raw material	Unit of measurement	Direct estimated cost savings per year	Indirect estimated cost savings per year	Total savings
TOTAL				

PRODUCTION

... The mechanical, electric, biological or chemical processes used to transform materials or information into products or services and deliver them to where they need to be. Offices, factories, farms and restaurants all rely upon equipment and machinery in one form or another to turn information and resources into goods and services and since many of these tools (and processes) can waste as much or more than they produce, they present a prime target for efficient, sustainable practices.

Interior analysis

Process map

1. Create a workable process map which identifies the significant process stages in your business's overall production system. (Note: service businesses can map system-process stages, supplier-chain stages, and/or customer-use stages.)

Process map analysis

2. Using your process map as a reference, identify and discuss with fellow employees how waste can be eliminated in several key stages. Examples of potential waste sources include, but are not limited to:

   - Equipment (extraneous, redundant, over-buying, etc.),
   - Transportation and/or delivery,
   - Energy use,
   - Raw materials,
   - Time,
   - Labour.

3. What did the discussions with your employees reveal?

Exterior analysis

Synergistic networks

4. Expand and broaden the *cooperative networking* information you collected in the *Processes* section by examining possible ways your business can become involved in a 'synergistic' industrial arrangement or 'industrial ecosystem'.

5. Explain *how* your business can achieve cost savings by setting up synergistic networks. Describe the estimated financial savings you envision as well as the costs involved.

Total: interior/exterior waste

Waste elimination (by unit)

6. Create a graph similar to the one below and record the amount of waste that your business estimates it can eliminate annually from its production processes.

Types of waste	Unit of measurement	Total amount eliminated (by unit) annually
Liquid:		
Solid:		
Gases:		
Other:		

Under each category (liquid, solid, etc.) list the specific names or types of waste you estimate will be eliminated.

Overall estimated **cost savings**

7. Create a graph similar to the one below and record your overall estimated cost-savings in each of the categories.

	Unit of measurement	Cost per unit	Units saved	Cost savings (per year)
Equipment				
Energy				
Raw materials				
Time				
Labour				
Other				

RESULTS

TOTAL: waste-elimination estimates

Total waste elimination (PLACE/PRODUCT/PRODUCTION)

1. Create a graph similar to the one below and record the total waste data that your business estimates it can eliminate annually from the Place, Product and Production categories.

Types of waste	Unit of measurement	Total amount eliminated (by unit) annually
Liquid:		
Solid:		
Gases:		
Other:		

Under each category (liquid, solid, etc.) list the specific names or types of waste you estimate will be eliminated.

TOTAL: estimated cost savings

TOTAL cost savings (PLACE/PRODUCT/PRODUCTION)

2. Add the *total* cost savings that your business estimates it can eliminate annually in the Place, Product and Production categories. Display the number prominently.

TOTAL: job security and job creation

Have your efforts produced job security or created jobs? Explain your answer.

TOTAL: Increases in productivity and revenues

Have your waste-elimination achievements produced overall increases in productivity and/or revenues? If so, record and display them in percentage form (e.g. we achieved a 14% increase in production, which helped bring about a 7% increase in revenues, or, our employees decreased the time normally required to process order forms by 28% ... which translates to an increase in revenues of 3.5%).

About the Authors

Jonathan T. Scott (www.jonathantscott.com) is a lecturer, manager, entrepreneur and business leader with over 25 years of work experience in eight different countries. As a manager he was recognized for tripling productivity, reducing costs by up to 40%, and increasing net profits by over 55% at the companies where he worked. In the process he conducted three separate turn-arounds (the first occurred in a war zone; the second was described as 'the best of its kind in the country') and pioneered multi-million-dollar projects in parts of the world where they previously did not exist. Currently, Scott runs a business-education business. He is also the founder and director of the *Center for Industrial Productivity and Sustainability* (www.cipsfoundation.com) and *Wind Gateway* (www.windgateway.com). He serves, or has served, at the following business schools: *Kozminski University* (Warsaw, Poland), the *Rotterdam School of Management* (The Netherlands), the *Audencia Nantes School of Management* (Nantes, France) and *Bradford University* (Bradford, UK). He has also taught at the *University of Perugia* (Italy). In 2009, he was presented with an 'outstanding achievements in teaching' award. Scott's education includes attending *Brevard College* (Brevard, North Carolina) before graduating with a BSc degree from (Tallahassee). He has studied at the *Université de Bourgogne* (Dijon, France), earned an MBA (in management) from Western International University (at its former London, UK campus), received a teaching certification from *Oxford Brookes University* (Oxford, UK), and secured an MA (in management) from *Kozminski University* (Warsaw, Poland). Scott is the author of the following books (four of which are award-winning): *Fundamentals of Leisure Business Success* (1998), *The Concise Handbook of Management* (2005), *Managing the New Frontiers* (2008), *The Entrepreneur's Guide to Building a Successful Business* (2009), *The Sustainable Business* (2010), *New Standards for Long-Term Business Survival* (2011) and the action/adventure novel *On Wings* (2007). His specialty subjects include management, entrepreneurship, and sustainability.

Walter R. Stahel (www.product-life.org) is the head of Risk Management at the *Geneva Association* (Switzerland), the insurance industry's most prestigious research body. He is also a respected business advisor and the founder and director of the *Product-Life Institute* (Geneva, Switzerland), Europe's oldest sustainability-based consultancy and think-tank. Stahel's pioneering research and collaborative work in the field of sustainability stretch back several decades – firmly establishing him as one of the subject's founders and appliers. He is a visiting professor at the Faculty of Engineering and Physical Sciences at the *University of Surrey* (UK) and is a regular guest lecturer (in the graduate department) at *Tohoku University* (Japan). Stahel is an alumnus of ETH, the Swiss Federal Institute of Technology (Zurich, Switzerland) and holds an honorary PhD from the University of Surrey. He is also the author of several prize-winning papers and pioneering academic books including: *Jobs for Tomorrow: The Potential for Substituting Manpower for Energy* (1976/1982), co-authored with Genevieve Reday; *The Limits of Certainty* (1989/1993), written with Orio Giarini and published in six languages; and *The Performance Economy* (2006/2010). He is a member of the Club of Rome.

For Product Safety Concerns and Information please contact our EU
representative GPSR@taylorandfrancis.com Taylor & Francis Verlag GmbH,
Kaufingerstraße 24, 80331 München, Germany

Printed and bound by CPI Group (UK) Ltd, Croydon, CR0 4YY

01/05/2025

01858326-0001